English Mastiff

The World's Heaviest Dog

by Dawn Bluemel Oldfield

Consultant: Jennifer Lambden
Secretary, Mastiff Club of America

BEARPORT
PUBLISHING

New York, New York

Credits

Cover, © Jagodka/Shutterstock; TOC, © Svetlana Golnikova/www.mastiffhills.com; 4–5, © Jerry Shulman/SuperStock/Alamy; 6, © Sergey Lavrentev/Shutterstock; 8, 9, © Svetlana Golnikova/www.mastiffhills.com; 10–11, © Jennifer Lambden/Sunnydale Mastiffs; 12, © Mary Evans Picture Library; 13, © Svetlana Golnikova/www.mastiffhills.com; 14, © Lee6713/Dreamstime; 15, 16, 17, © Svetlana Golnikova/www.mastiffhills.com; 18, 19, © L. Ackerman, Cimbri Mastiffs, TX-USA; 20, © Svetlana Golnikova/www.mastiffhills.com; 21, © Jerry Shulman/SuperStock/Alamy; 22L, © Fedor Selivanov/Shutterstock; 22C, © Liliya Kulianionak/Shutterstock; 22R, © Vera Zinkova/Shutterstock; 23TL, © Sibrikov Valery/Shutterstock; 23TR, © L. Ackerman, Cimbri Mastiffs, TX-USA; 23BL, © Svetlana Golnikova/www.mastiffhills.com; 23BR, © Meirion Matthias/Shutterstock.

Publisher: Kenn Goin
Senior Editor: Joyce Tavolacci
Creative Director: Spencer Brinker
Photo Researcher: Calcium Creative

Library of Congress Cataloging-in-Publication Data

Bluemel Oldfield, Dawn.
 English mastiff : the world's heaviest dog / by Dawn Bluemel Oldfield.
    pages cm. — (Even more supersized!)
 Audience: 6-9.
 Includes bibliographical references and index.
 ISBN 978-1-61772-728-3 (library binding) — ISBN 1-61772-728-8 (library binding)
 1. Mastiff—Juvenile literature. I. Title.

SF429.M36B58 2013
636.73—dc23

2012035912

For more information, write to Bearport Publishing Company, Inc., 45 West 21st Street, Suite 3B, New York, New York 10010. Printed in the United States of America.

10 9 8 7 6 5 4 3 2 1

Contents

Heavyweight

The English mastiff is the heaviest dog in the world.

An English mastiff weighs about as much as a refrigerator.

A male English mastiff weighs between 150 and 250 pounds (68 and 113 kg). A female weighs between 120 and 200 pounds (54 and 91 kg).

An Ancient Dog

Mastiffs were first raised in Asia around 5,000 years ago.

About 2,000 years ago, people brought the large, strong dogs to England.

The mastiffs were trained to help English soldiers fight their enemies.

The dogs wore **armor** and spiked collars in battle.

The very first mastiffs are thought to have come from a part of Asia called Tibet.

Tibetan mastiff

Where English Mastiffs Were First Raised

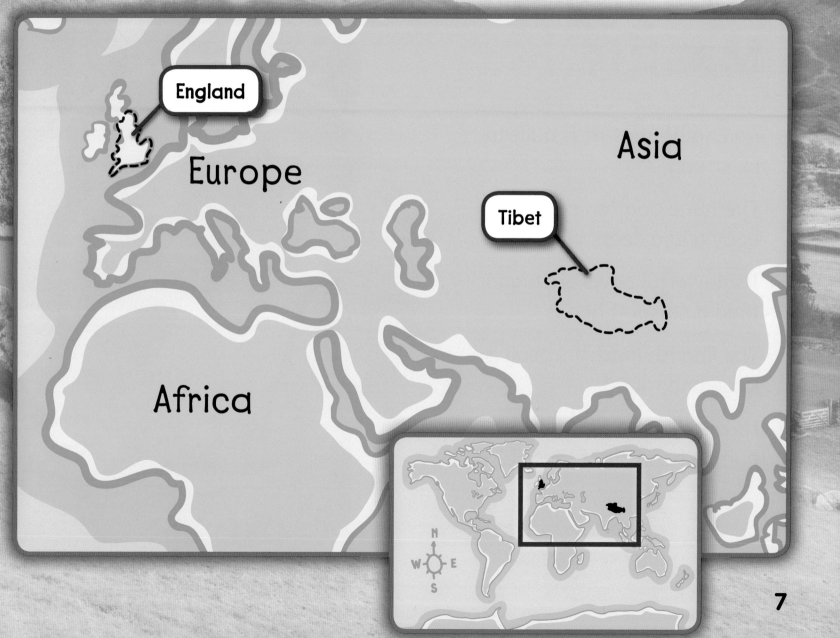

The Mighty Mastiff

An English mastiff is built to be strong.

The huge dog has a long, tall body and a deep, wide chest.

Its powerful paws are bigger than a person's hands.

The English mastiff's head is large and round.

Its mouth is so big that a human head can fit inside!

paw

An adult English mastiff can grow to be about 30 inches (76 cm) tall at the shoulder.

large head

long body

wide chest

At Work

Because it is so big and strong, the English mastiff was used as a working dog.

People trained the mastiff to hunt huge animals, such as bears.

The giant dog was also used to pull small carts and haul heavy loads.

During World War I (1914–1918), soldiers used English mastiffs to pull carts filled with weapons to the battlefield.

mastiffs
pulling carts

On Guard

English mastiffs are not just strong, they are also brave and loyal.

Mastiffs will protect their owner's home and family from danger.

They let out a deep, loud bark if a stranger comes near.

Despite their fierce bark, mastiffs are usually gentle and friendly.

guard dog

For thousands of years, mastiffs guarded castles and homes. They also kept wolves and other dangerous animals away from sheep and other **livestock**.

Family Dog

English mastiffs are sweet dogs that love spending time with people.

Mastiffs are known for being calm and getting along well with other pets and children.

However, owners should always watch their giant dogs around small kids.

One wag of the dogs' huge tails can easily knock over a young child.

English mastiffs are nicknamed "gentle giants" because of their sweet personalities.

Happy and Healthy

Caring for an English mastiff is no small job.

Owners need to teach their big, heavy dogs not to jump up on people and knock them down.

English mastiffs also need a home with lots of space to run and play.

Like people, mastiffs need **exercise** each day to stay fit and healthy.

Some English mastiffs slobber, or drool. Owners should have a towel ready to clean up the wet mess.

Puppy Power

English mastiffs grow up to be very large dogs, yet they start out small.

Mastiff puppies weigh only about two pounds (1 kg) when they are born.

Like other newborn puppies, they cannot see or walk.

For the first few weeks of their lives, they sleep and drink their mother's milk.

At eight weeks old, the puppies are ready to become part of a human family.

A female English mastiff usually has a **litter** of four to twelve puppies.

puppies

Living Large

It doesn't take long for mastiff puppies to become giants of the dog world.

At only six months old, the young dogs can weigh about 100 pounds (45 kg).

That's as much as a baby hippo!

They are fully grown at around two years of age.

By then, these giants have shown their owners just how loving and loyal they are.

three-month-old puppy

More Heavy Dogs

English mastiffs are part of a large group of animals called mammals. Almost all mammals give birth to live young instead of laying eggs. The babies drink milk from their mothers. Mammals are also warm-blooded and most have hair or fur on their skin.

Here are three more heavy dogs.

Saint Bernard

The Saint Bernard is the world's second heaviest dog. It can weigh up to 200 pounds (91 kg).

Newfoundland

A Newfoundland is a large, strong dog that can weigh as much as 150 pounds (68 kg).

Irish Wolfhound

The Irish wolfhound is one of the tallest and heaviest dogs in the world. It can weigh up to 125 pounds (57 kg).

English Mastiff
250 pounds/113 kg

Saint Bernard
200 pounds/91 kg

Newfoundland
150 pounds/68 kg

Irish Wolfhound
125 pounds/57 kg

Glossary

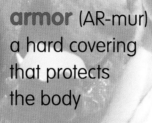

armor (AR-mur) a hard covering that protects the body

litter (LIT-ur) a group of baby animals that are born to the same mother at the same time

exercise (EX-sur-syez) an activity to stay fit and healthy, such as running

livestock (LIVE-stok) animals, such as sheep and cows, that are raised by people on farms or ranches

Index

Read More

Furstinger, Nancy. *Mastiffs.* Minneapolis, MN: ABDO (2006).

Landau, Elaine. *Mastiffs are the Best!* Minneapolis, MN: Lerner (2011).

Nelson, Maria. *Mastiffs (Great Big Dogs).* New York: Gareth Stevens (2011).

Learn More Online

To learn more about English mastiffs, visit
www.bearportpublishing.com/EvenMoreSuperSized